To Amy, Debbie, Treva, Barbie, Brionna, and Katie, thank you for being my second family and including me in your Christmas baking weekend. What wonderful gifts you make and give back to the community.

To Tianna, I'm always so proud of you.

To Timeko, may you never stop using your love of popcorn to make others smile.

Giving Gal Press

Text copyright © by Stephanie L. Jones and Giving Gal, LLC.

Illustrations copyright © by Stephanie L. Jones and Giving Gal, LLC.

The Giving Gal name and character are trademarks of Giving Gal, LLC.

All rights reserved. No part of this book may be used or reproduced in any manner whatsoever without written permission except in the case of brief quotations in articles or reviews.

For information about bulk purchase discounts or bringing Stephanie to a live event, please contact Stephanie L. Jones at 219-707-9545 or Stephanie@GivingGal.com.

Visit www.GivingGal.com or www.GivingGalbooks.com for additional information.

Manufactured in the U.S.A.

ISBN: 978-1-948693-15-8 (paperback), 978-1-948693-16-5 (hardback), 978-1-948693-13-4 (audiobook), 978-1-948693-14-1 (epub)

LOC: Library of Congress Control Number: 2022910496

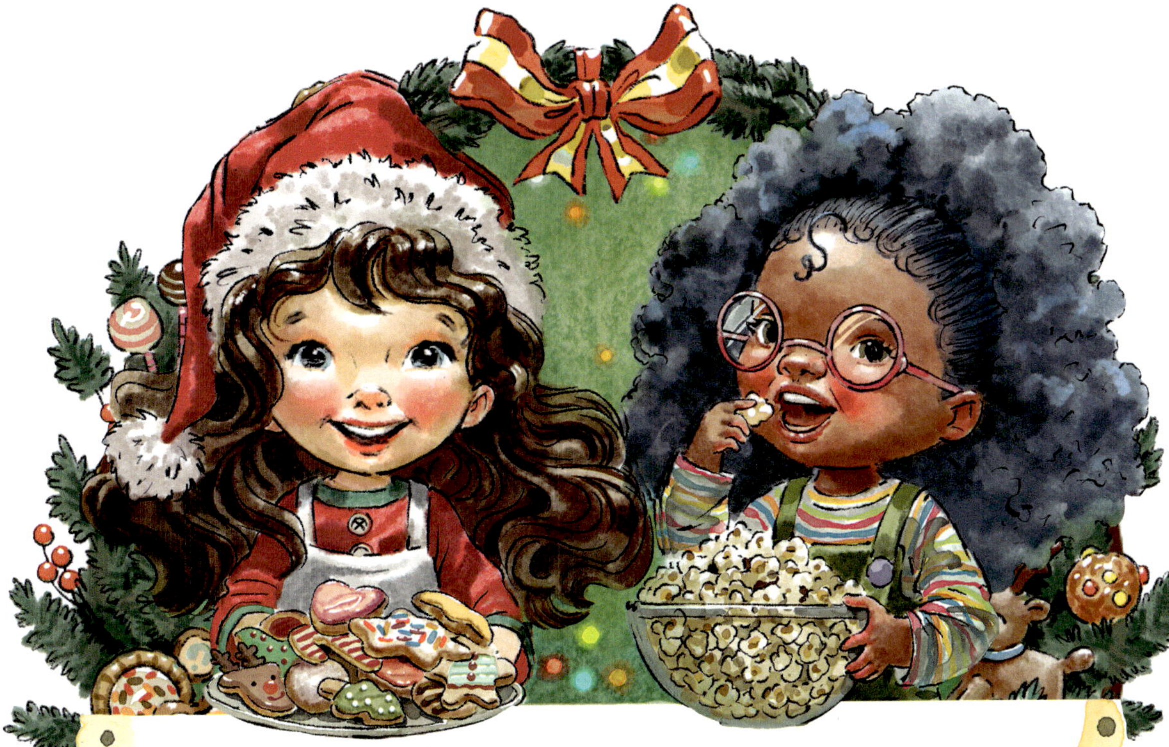

GIVING GAL
and the
Christmas Cookie Extravaganza

Illustrator
Angelina Valieva

Author
Stephanie L. Jones

"Rise and shine, my little Giving Gal,"
Gabi's mom whispered.
"Today's the Christmas Cookie Extravaganza.
Our annual tradition!"

"What's a tradition?"

"A tradition is an activity or event
we do each year."

Giving Gal put on
her favorite holiday T-shirt,
slid into her reindeer slippers,
and placed a Santa hat on her head.

"Festive! I look so festive!"

One by one, friends arrived.

Giving Gal gave everyone a big hug while her older sister, Grace, took their coats.

Giving Gal loved all of her friends, but she kept peeking out the window for her new friend, Tianna, to arrive.

Where could she be? Is she coming?

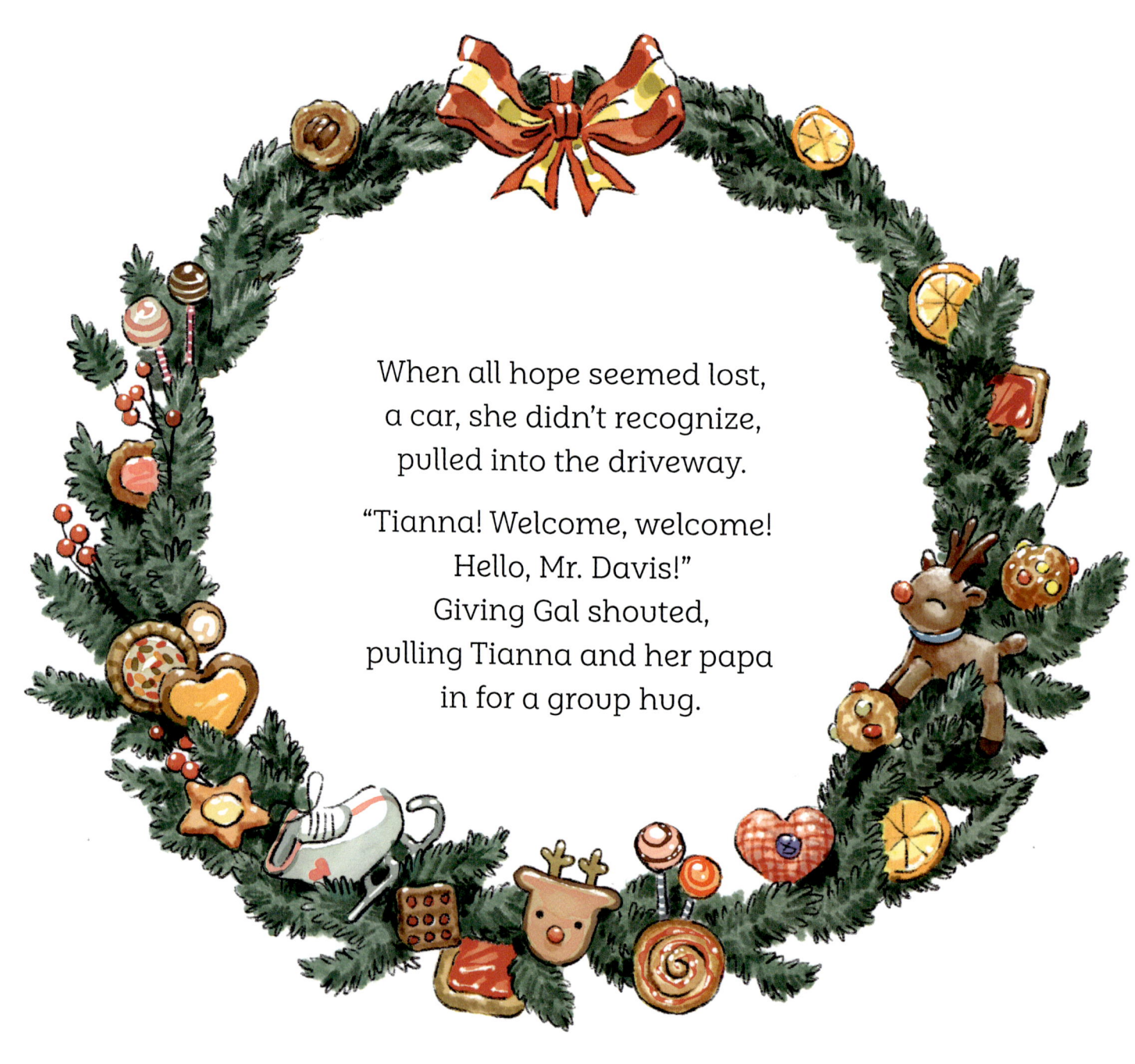

When all hope seemed lost,
a car, she didn't recognize,
pulled into the driveway.

"Tianna! Welcome, welcome!
Hello, Mr. Davis!"
Giving Gal shouted,
pulling Tianna and her papa
in for a group hug.

"Okay, friend, here's how our Christmas Cookie Extravaganza works. Everyone has a job."

"I will take you around, show you the jobs, and you pick what you would like to do."

"Easy peasy!" Giving Gal said.

Brionna and her mom Debbie rolled cookie dough into balls.

"Tianna, want to help?" Brionna asked.

"No. I'm no good at rolling cookie dough into balls. They always turn out lumpy."

"Who cares if they're lumpy?" Giving Gal exclaimed. "I bet they will still be yummy!"

Amy and her Aunt Treva dipped cake balls in melted chocolate.

"Tianna, want to help?" Amy asked.

"No. I'm no good at dipping. I'll make a mess with the chocolate."

"Who cares if you make a mess?" Giving Gal said.
"We can always clean it up."

Carlos and his cousin Arona flattened the cookie dough with a rolling pin.

"Tianna, want to help?" Carlos asked.

"No. I'm no good at rolling dough. I'm not strong enough."

"You are stronger than you think!" Giving Gal cheered.
"I'm sure Carlos would help you."

Giving Gal's mom and Grace decorated the cookies with colorful icing.

"Tianna, want to help us decorate the cookies?" Grace asked.

"No. I'm no good at decorating cookies. I'm not very artsy."

"You are very creative," Giving Gal encouraged. "Remember the card you made for Mrs. Lemon? She loved it!"

"Tianna," Giving Gal hollered. "Come help me string popcorn to wrap around the tree."

"Popcorn!" Tianna squealed. "I love popcorn!"

"I love popping popcorn!"

"I love eating popcorn!"

"And I love making popcorn decorations!"

"Yippee!" Giving Gal shouted.

"See, Tianna, we all have something we are good at. It's okay you are not the best at rolling, dipping, and decorating. You are amazing with anything popcorn!"

"Thanks for all of the encouragement you gave me today, Giving Gal. You never gave up on finding me an activity I could do."

"That's what friends are for, Tianna. Or should I call you the Popcorn Queen, P.Q. for short?" Giving Gal laughed.

"I'm so grateful you came over for the annual Christmas Cookie Extravaganza," Giving Gal said. "The day would not have been the same without you. And if you had fun today, just wait for our annual Valentine's Card Making Day!"

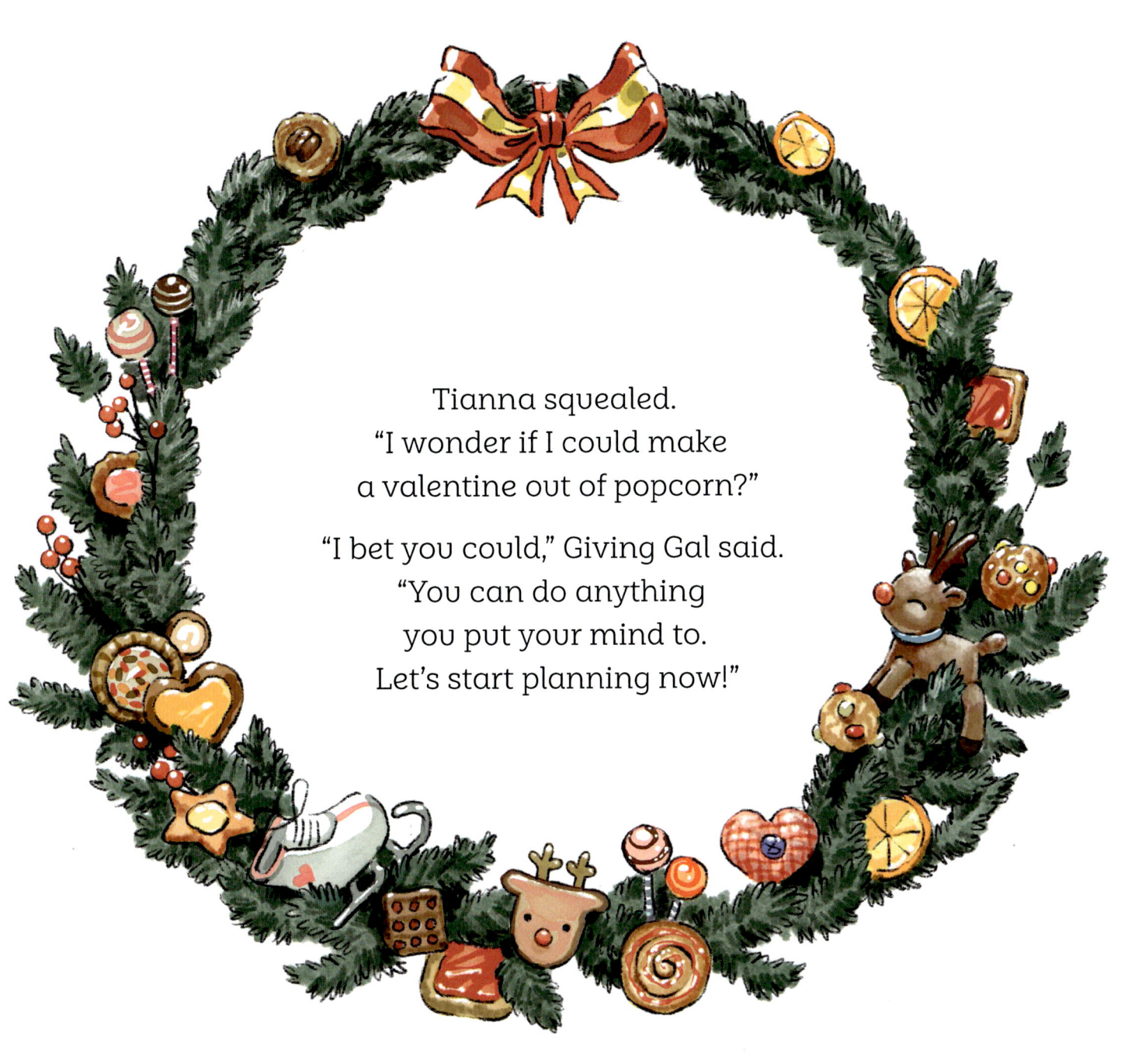

Tianna squealed.
"I wonder if I could make
a valentine out of popcorn?"

"I bet you could," Giving Gal said.
"You can do anything
you put your mind to.
Let's start planning now!"

Meet the real-life Christmas Cookie Extravaganza crew!

If you liked this book, you may also like the first book in the Giving Gal™ series.

www.GivingGalBooks.com

A Special Note for Parents, Caregivers, and Teachers

In a "What gift am I receiving for Christmas?" world, we have an opportunity to shape the future by raising children to be kind, encouraging, compassionate, and giving.

As you read this book together, have your child identify how the children tried to involve Tianna and the ways Giving Gal™ attempted to encourage her. Talk with your child about the power of encouragement and how we can raise others up by focusing on what they can do and not what they can't.

For engaging activities for churches, teachers, and parents,
visit www.GivingGalBooks.com.

This book gives back. Each year, with your help, we'll select several nonprofits to donate a portion of the proceeds from this book.

About the Author   Stephanie L. Jones

Stephanie L. Jones is on a mission to inspire others to give and practice gratitude daily. She loves sharing her message in schools, churches, and with companies. Besides her children's book, *Giving Gal*™, she's an award-winning author of *The Giving Challenge*, *The Gratitude Challenge*, and *Thank-You Notes to God*. She lives out her dreams with her hubby, Mike.

About the Illustrator   Angelina Valieva

Born into a family of artists, Angelina's father directed her hand and taught her to draw. Her children's book illustrations have been published worldwide. In addition, she's successfully participated in international art competitions.